tacenda at eventide © 2022 Victoria Tan

All rights reserved.

No part of this publication may be reproduced, stored in a retrieval system, or transmitted, in any form or by any means, electronic, mechanical, photocopying, recording or otherwise, without the prior written permission of the presenters.

Victoria Tan asserts the moral right to be identified as author of this work.

Presentation by *BookLeaf Publishing*

Web: www.bookleafpub.com

E-mail: info@bookleafpub.com

ISBN: 9789357690294

First edition 2022

AF795802

tacenda at eventide

Victoria Tan

BookLeaf Publishing

what comes from the heartwood

the moments i still have
of you
are solidified golden,
like amber,
suspended in a drop of resin
for all eternity,
unchanging.

like
the first time
you embraced me
by the yellow buses,
standing on rough pavement,
under the blazing
almost-summer
sun.

my face
pressed into your white shirt
and the fragrance of laundry detergent,
your chin hovering above the crown of my
head,
how we knocked into each other
when i pulled back;
your laugh
as you pretended
to be hurt.

i have never
pretended to be hurt—
i have pretended

that i was not;
because in those
amber memories,
only your words
and the absence of them
could crack me open.

that is not to say
you were cruel.
quite the opposite:
you were kind
and tried to show care.
but,
behind a gold resin mask
was supreme indifference.

it was not always amber,
the things i remember of us.
sometimes,
it was lovely-dark,
like late evening drifting into deep night,
and our conversations

blue-lit
on a screen.

and when those moments
dredge up like smooth black stones
from twilight shallows,
they bring with them
paintbrush shades
of what you thought into being,
tapped onto a keyboard,
and how there was
adoration
in printed white text.

then i think
perhaps you did hold affection,
but it was not strong enough
to reach past the walls
of yourself.
which meant
the tiny ephemeral thing
i thought protected in amber
was simply

fossilized,
well-arranged,
dust.

but i will never know.
because to ask
would shatter fragile amber
and strip away lovely darkness,
and i cannot bear to think
that
after all,
there was nothing
within.

an elegy to paper cranes

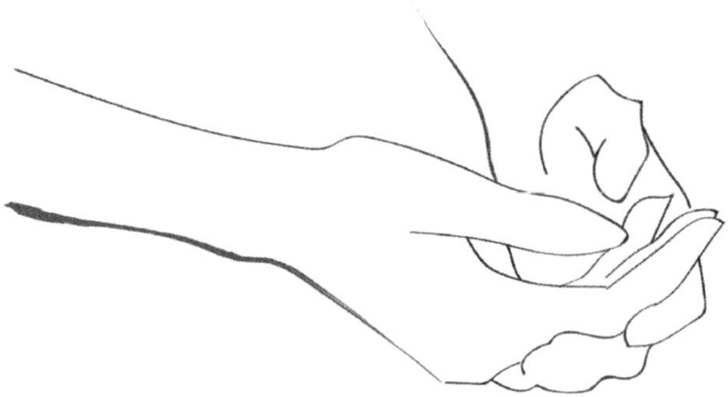

cranes,
that you gave me,
paper and folded from every color,
wings bound to hempen thread, dangling,
and clustered together in your palm as you
offered it outwards.
if this was a story i could say your
expression was hopeful,
but this is not a story
and your expression was inscrutable.

(only your eyes came alive, wide and
curious,
perhaps searching my face for that elusive
something
as i was yours.)

to describe what lingered between us
would be like watching fireflies at dusk,
there
and gone
and there again,
winking light hazy through the evening
shade.
the memory of it comes in heat waves,
golden days and discordant nights,
stolen glances across a room.

i took the cranes,
their hidden thoughtful messages written
in small cramped script,
and sometimes i wonder if that was a
mistake,

if by that small acceptance i also took
from you your affection,
or perhaps not,
and you never cared at all.

from then on, we did not speak.
stolen glances became a dance of
avoidance,
golden days turned to burnt afternoons,
discordant nights melted to aching silence.
the question i turned over in my mind,
like a tailor inspecting torn silk,
was whether i had given my heart to you,
and all you handed back was a set of paper
cranes.

sometimes i caught your dark eyes on
mine,
and i would wonder.
then you spoke to another,
so i ceased to wonder, folding my hope in
my chest
like the petals of a dying flower.

(yet even in your conversation,
you were wholly without desire,
only she, like me,
leaning in to your attention.)
now cranes gather dust,
some messages left unopened,
half-abandoned,
like the end to us.
but still,
today,
you bowed your head to me in
acknowledgment,
and perhaps,
that is enough
for the two of us.

telephone lines

a handful of thin black brushstrokes
stark on a gainsboro sky:
cable strung overhead, and
three dark birds perched
on high
wire.

lines running parallel and crossing,
clustered on weathered wood poles,
carrying the invisible
intangible
weightless

sparking currents of electricity
connecting you to me
and me to you.

the rustle of the wind in autumn-parched
leaves,
rough scrapes of pavement under shoe
soles,
skin numbed by chill,
the thought
i want to hang
that blows away like
dandelion fluff.

me to you and you to me,
dark-bright screens reading
9:30—
then you're gone.
rewind.
sparks jump backwards across telephone
lines

to flushed cheeks,
fingers skittering across keys,
and moonstruck message after message
sent:
contemporary letter-writing.
what you and me and me and you lacked
for—
reams of parchment and swan-feather
quills,
iron gall ink and liveried messengers
riding up on gallant bay steeds—
was made up for by words.
archaic language
of long-dead poets,
18th century,
in the mouths and hands of
15, 16 year-olds,
crossing air and miles apart
through telephone lines.

above my head,
cables that merge together.
sun's gone, cloud-cover,

but now,
what i remember most of all,
is how you bloom
under the sunlight.

wire strung bleak along stretches of blank
time,
like you and me,
letters unsent,
in the absence of energy.
and above my head,
on the long walk home,
telephone lines,
that diverge.

garden half-dead, half-mine

gray, green, gray.
stretches of blank time and
a garden.
march when it budded,
april and may to blossom
june to ripen
july and august to stagnate,
september to wither.

gray,
and the art of willful ignoring.
green,
and you said
how long we have waited for things long
ago
to come unravel.
gray,
and i remember how you let
everything slip through your fingers
like water.

the excuses that
you made:
not favoring conversation,
books over love,
the tumultuous riptide of your nature,
how it was not your wish
to cultivate a garden—
and yet,
you wished to pick
its roses.

and how i have only ever been half to you.
half in your thoughts,
half with you and
half away,
half-important,
half a lover,
half yours.

when golden hour stretches long

when golden hour stretches long,
i think of us.
the taste of sun and strawberry, like
artificial flavor in my mouth,
a pink lollipop between your lips,
the two of us haloed by gold light

in a half-empty classroom.
lingering affection
spoken through the way you said my
name.
the buzz of electricity
in my veins where we touch,
interlocking fingers.

i cannot be the only lover ever
to have dreamt illusions of us,
like my head pillowed in your lap,
doing homework in the quiet dusk of
evening,
lamp-lit in a room,
wrapped in the bliss of secure love.
and i cannot be the only lover ever
left with only this in my hands:
the imprint and impression
of fading sunlight.

to be ruined (to be gone)

this
is what a ruination feels like.
this is heartbreak.
this is the eye of the storm
and the reckoning of the war to end all
wars
and the mutually assured destruction
of you and him
and everything you know.

and it isn't glass shattering.
it's cutting your fingers on shards
as you crawl through the debris
to piece them back together.
it's clutching a clipped rosebud
and wishing in vain
to reverse the cut from its stem,
it's trying to hold rain as it slips through
your fingers
and trying to catch dandelion fluff
blowing away in the wind.
it's being lost in the bleakest of deep
nights
without the hope of daybreak
to guide you out of the woods.

and it isn't your heart breaking.
it's your rib cage caving in on itself
from the force of your devastation,
legs weakening and head ringing.
it isn't begging.
it's a prayer at his feet,
it's a psalm to whatever gods are out there,

it’s you on your knees clutching at his legs
and beseeching him
with all that you have in your soul:
don’t go. don’t go.

and then it’s watching him leave anyway.
it's his gentle touch on your hands
as he pulls away
and walks out of your life.
it's the door closing behind his retreating
form,
without a glance backwards.
and it’s crumbling alone in a dark desolate
room,
it’s sinking beneath inky waves and
wanting to drown.
it’s the lightning strike above,
the last thing you’ll ever see
before you are
gone.

where the wild things sing

i have spoken to the moon,
and gloried in its frost-shivering light.
i have heard the voice of the sea,
and watched the sun kiss liquid gold into
its depths.
i know where the wild things sing;

i have gone down to the earth's deep forges
and walked paths of twisted metal hymns.

now i whisper stars into existence,
and scatter their crushed-glass glory over
deep night.
i have raised grinding black cliffs of
knife-blade mountains,
and swept away the dust of stone from
their hidden flames.
i have seen the making of the world,
and the twined harmony of all the things
within—
so now i shall go,
and i go to where the wild things sing.

let the weather speak

i long for a storm
to match this shaking rage within:
for the earth to tear from its foundations
of cold dark stone,
and the sky to shatter black

between splinters of lightning,
diamond-like.

and should the rain fall,
why,
then i would long for the damp rich scent
of a blossoming ground:
that petrichor in my nose and
silver lines over skin
to hide my tears.

and even should the skies clear,
and peel back the terrible darkness, the
mournful gray,
why,
then i think i would long for the brilliant
blue of euphoria
and the glory of heaven's arched vault,
beneath which lesser beings dance,
carried by the wind.
so do not look into my eyes, for they carry
not my soul;

rather gaze towards the sky and all its
elements.
and should you say
your heart is intemperate—
it is,
and as the weather speaks,
i am.

once and future glory

It can be said,
That the ruins of their palaces and our cities do not unmake a civilization,
Yet phoenix it, so mortal minds may make what they like of the past.
These ruins that we bury are the ruins we long for:

Trembling ethereality, wild tearing of
crumbling stone and overgrown
Life that is no life, the green on gray and
Glories between, what wonders we make
of gaps in the walls,
The stoic grandeur we imagine, we
fantasize.
See what beauties must have blossomed in
cracks,
See what splendors had been inscribed on
stones,
Their monuments of towers, bridges,
fallen arches, crumbling columns,
Ah, gone to nothing.
This quiet ruin is simply
The imprint of what had
Flourished into being.

sacer: all the glory and grief in the world

It shall be yours,
All the glory and grief in the world.
I welcome you, divine one,
With eld and stirrings of the north.
Wake now, divine one,
I go, I go,
And cleanse myself of taint.

Illumined, I see:
Dawn nears, divine one,
With terrible beauties and quicksilver souls.
I am, I am,
Your sacer, divine one,
And bloom beneath your morn.

my heart, you

my heart like thundering rain, beloved;
and you are not with me.
i fell in love with a poet
(i fell in love with you)
to my eternal joy and sorrow.
your words were too beautiful for this
world;
and so they were lies;
and so that is all we ever shall be.
my heart is a small and lovely and sad
thing
that i have given you to hold in your
hands.
and now i am beautiful and broken and
alone

in the cold air of your absence.
i miss you (i love you [i miss you])

to the little things (and you most of all)

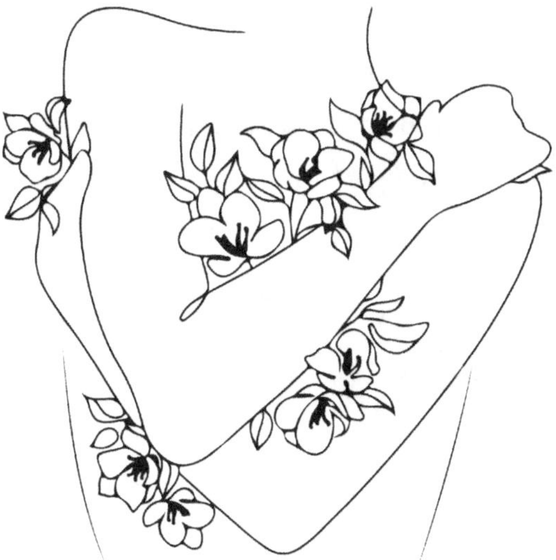

you have thrown your lot in with the
darkness,
but in your eyes, darling, is all the light we
cannot see.

you are the infinitely beautiful thing that
exists;
wondrous and glorious beyond measure.
i am drunk on you: the whiskey that is you
and your eyes,
your voice, your soul.
so raise a glass!
to the little things in life,
and to you most of all:
most precious, most extraordinary,
most deserving of love.

i am on the black cliffs

i am on the black cliffs, through the sea,
mist below and death above me.
i am where triumphs bloom and dawns are found,
follow me, follow me, follow me down.
i am with gods and glories abound,
seek infinite wonders among threads unwound.
i am in the stars, i am the storm,
follow me, follow me, into the morn.

all the skies and seas of love

words are wind,
as i well know from your empty praises
sung.
you are unmoved by mine own,
so i will let the weather speak in my stead.
my eyes are full of the tears i cannot shed;

i will let the sky weep for me instead.
all the sea would not be enough to drown
my sorrow.
all the sky would not be enough to free me
from my chains:
the ones i willingly put myself in for you.
and it is for you,
all for you.

i have barred the
way to my heart
(so you cannot
find me)

i can still feel my love for you knocking
at a small, dusty, windowless corner of my
heart,
but i will not let it in anymore.
i will not let you in anymore.
and one day, this knocking will quiet,
and fade,
and leave me,
just as you did.

i'm falling for your eyes (the truest thing i know)

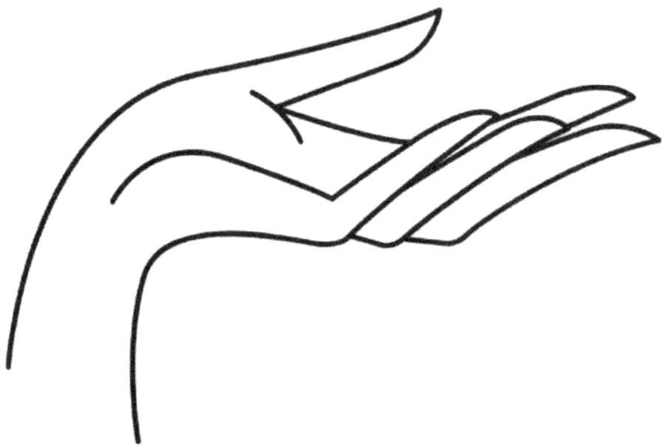

Shall the splendor of twilight be
dismissed?
By a dream of beauty (your eyes),
Held and hailed in mine own secret heart.
(Avail, me—)

In all the world; you, some sort of lover
like the storm.
Sung sweet at the first, then shunned,
I, hand outstretched,
Was turned away from thee.
Does the morning glory fade when
confronted with the sun?
And yet still, I believe (hope against
hope),
The windswept sea and the intemperate
sky would pale,
Against the mikrokosmos in your eyes.
Carry the dim pearl-light of dusk in your
dark eyes,
And when you smile (glory be)—
Let thine wonder; let it bring the dawn.

for all the ages (until the end of time)

We are all of us made of nothing more
than memories and stardust.
Yet I only remember you,
the brightest of them all.
I will love you
until the stars run out,

and even past then;
even when the void rushes in to swallow
us whole
and we are but faded shadows of our once
and future glory,
I will love you.

death and divinity (follow us closely)

Two titans stand at either end, amongst shattered stars
Under the empty blank sky, like a vacant vault,
A hollowness of blue beating damning and true,

Above the ones who are restless and tired,
The ones who are only human.

The mortals around them, wholly without the blood of gods,
Wage petty wars and clashes of steel,
Salt on their lips, blood on their hands,
Desperate defiance in their eyes
Ghosts of a ruined city clinging to their backs like shadows.

And still those titans wait,
For they have been circling each other for a long time.
Patience is in their veins where blood should be,
Alongside gold, eternally, infinitely slow,
Ancient as the dragging of the tide.

It must be very silent; it must be very still,
To be such a being—
In the hours that pass, the days that slip by,

Filled with the things one needs not say,
Of tragic gods, and these mortalities.

so rivers run (past the brink, past the)

There is a river that runs silver and cold,
Through steep dark banks and caves of old,
Flowing into our cups as starlight and wine,
There is a river, and we named it time.

There is a river of indigo and ink,
Into forests and vales, at last to the brink,
Taking a course from love to betrayal,
There is a river, we named it our fable.

There is a river that runs gold and green,
With wild light dancing, shining between,

Forward, in it earth's splendor and strife,
There is a river, and we named it life.

permutatio

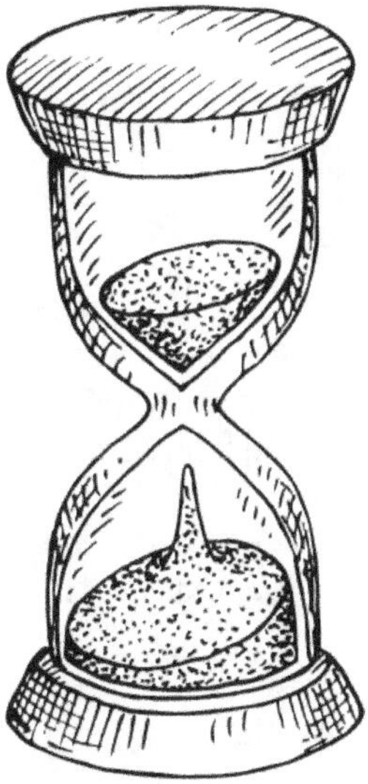

In the end,
Time runs out of clocks,
Seas froth and boil and run
Onto the torn land,
Our glories turn to ash in our mouths;
For storms are a-gathering, and I am at its
helm.

And in the end,
Worlds run past the ends of the earth,
As empires crumble and,
Desire taints the hearts and,
Life, inevitably, runs out.

And in the end,
It falls upon the shoulders of humans
without wings,
And altogether without splendor,
To bear us up,
Bear us past the past, past the end,
Past that which is unceasing, unchanging;
Forever unknowing.

And past the end,
Look to the harbinger, I, through these
silent things;
And mine bugles and fluttering cloth
proclaim:
"Past the joy, past the sun,
Transform, forerun, become."

phoenix(ed)

the barest flicker;
no more than a glint, really,
through buried ash in ash, through
gathered dust on dust,

again, it stirs,
gold
or any color against gray

broken-singed, broken-faithed
and yet, still,
so, so beautiful

it brightens, alight;
phoenix, phoenixed
nothing gold—goes to ash, to rise